I0123324

THE DAY AFTER THE FUNERAL

What to Say to Those Who Grieve

Praise for an earlier version of this book,
How to Write Comforting Letters to the Bereaved

As one who professionally interacts with dying and bereaved persons regularly, I find this guide to be an immediate help to me at multiple levels. Not only does it help with writing to bereft survivors, it even helps with what to say to them when stranded in that awkward silence in person or on the phone. I heartily recommend it to professionals and volunteers who might struggle for a sincere voice of caring. This guide most certainly takes a permanent place among my references.

> **—Diane R. Morrison, LCSW**
> Kaiser Permanente
> Los Angeles Medical Center

ॐ

John Haley's guide, *How to Write Comforting Letters to the Bereaved*, is as comforting and supportive as the letter we would hope to receive in times of loss and bereavement. For all who might wish aid in writing and comforting a friend, relative or colleague, Haley's guide is a spur to the imagination and a practical set of guidelines to express what is in your heart.

> **—Alan Briskin, Ph.D.**
> Co-author of *Daily Miracles: Humanity and Excellence in Health Care*
> Oakland, CA

ॐ

How to Write Comforting Letters to the Bereaved makes a great contribution.

—John D. Morgan, PhD.
King's College
Centre for Education about Death and Bereavement
London, Ontario Canada

❦

How to Write Comforting Letters to the Bereaved reflects true insight and sensitivity. The book should be a very practical, down-to-earth help for many who wish to express sympathy and comfort through the written word. Thank you for writing it.

—The Rev. Carl Malm
Grief Counselor, Center for Loss, Grief and Change
Huntsville, AL

❦

THE DAY AFTER THE FUNERAL
What to Say to Those Who Grieve

ISBN 978-1-938842-76-4
Copyright© 2025 John D. Haley, M.A.

All rights reserved. No part of this book may be reprinted or reproduced, or utilized in any form or by any electronic, mechanical, or other means, now known or hereafter invented, including photocopying and recording, or in any information storage or retrieval system, without permission in writing from the publisher.

Published by Bardolf & Company
www.bardolfandcompany.com

An earlier verison, *How to Write Comforting Letters to the Bereaved,* was first published in 2002 by the Baywood Publishing Company, Inc., Amityville, NY. Subsequently, it was published in 2018 by Routledge, Milton Park, United Kingdom, and New York, USA.

Cover design: Cathleen Shaw, Shaw Creative Group

Notice: Product or corporate names may be trademarks or registered trademarks, and are used only for identification and explanation without intent to infringe.

Dedication

To my wife, Adrianne,
with more gratitude than words can express,
for sharing this loopy rollercoaster ride called life.

And to all who have ever offered a shoulder
or lent an ear to a suffering family member,
friend, colleague, or even a stranger,
in peacetime or war.
You have helped make the world a little softer,
one heart at a time.

Also by John Haley

"How to Write Letters of Comfort to the Bereaved."
The Director, the official organ of the National Funeral
Directors Association. NFDA Publications, Inc.
March/April, 1982.

"Compassion on Paper." *Signs of the Times.* Pacific Press
Publishing Association, a Seventh-day Adventist Institution.
December, 1988.

"Our Two Grandfathers." *Old Huntsville: History and Stories
of the Tennessee Valley.* Old Huntsville, Inc.
April, 2016.

"Launching Together: Rocket City and Me." *Rocket City.*
Huntsville-Madison County Public Library.
2019.

THE DAY AFTER THE FUNERAL

What to Say to Those Who Grieve

John Haley, M.A.

Bardolf & Company
Sarasota, Florida

Contents

The Day After the Funeral

Has your pen ever hovered above a blank page, or have your fingertips frozen above the keyboard or phone screen, while you puzzle about what to say to someone who has experienced the death of a loved one? Have you felt that this time the sympathy card alone, or the tweet, or a social media post would not be enough? If so, would you like help finding your voice to lend support?

Whether the recipient is family or friend, parishioner or patient, client or customer, the suggestions herein can help when that empty space stares back at you. With this guide, you will learn how to draw on your knowledge and experience to create unique, personalized messages in writing, in conversation, or in recordings. You can find new ways to beam light across the dark chasm of permanent loss—light enriched with individual meaning and restorative power.

You may even help heal yourself.

What You'll Find Here

Between the covers of *The Day After the Funeral*, you will find:

- *An understanding* of how grief and bereavement can be approached in simple, straightforward terms, without heavy, academic jargon. In writing and conversation.

- *Frequently asked questions* with practical answers and real examples of ways to express yourself in a variety of situations.

- *Scripting ideas* for reels or videos drawn from the above answers and examples.

- *An easy-to-use format* that lets you jump straight to questions of highest interest.

- *Suggestions* for addressing a broad spectrum of occurrences—from the tranquil passing of an elderly parent to highly sensitive circumstances like suicide, tragic auto accident, combat, or stillborn child.

- *Reflections* on faith and religion—ways to address the subject and when to leave it alone.

- *Actions* you can take in addition to the written or recorded message.

- *Encouragement* to overcome reluctance to reach out to someone who is grieving, especially if you think others will neglect them.

- *Insights* into the nature of grief itself, for the benefit of others and perhaps even your own.

13

Which Is Better:
Cards & Letters Or Social Media?

The array of communication options in modern life may require different approaches when reaching out to the grieving. Some people only dabble in social media every month or so, or even never. Others seem smitten with it, as if it matters more than the air they breathe. Neither choice is innately superior to the other. However, when seeking to comfort someone in bleak circumstances, it helps to be mindful of these communication preferences.

For those who prefer low-tech, make a point to send traditional cards, notes, or letters. They will appreciate the familiar touch of something tangible, rather than the cyber touch of keystrokes and flat, glaring screens. Everything about electronic communications connotes "speed," "instantaneous," and, by implication, "don't have time." By contrast, everything about death conveys "infinity," "permanence," and, by implication, the "preciousness of the time we share." If you reach out to a grieving family member, friend, or colleague only through social media, his or her reaction may not be one of appreciation for the speed of response, but one of "Is this all my loss is worth to you?"

Conversely, for a high-tech communicator, conveying your thoughts and feelings by email, text messages, or other platforms or apps is much more likely to be perceived as "griever-friendly." Not only does your first message arrive quickly, but it could well initiate back-and-forth sharing that builds upon itself more fluidly than traditional correspondence. These methods also have the potential to carry more than your individual perspective; with a few extra clicks, you can attach links to websites or videos that have helpful information applicable to the recipient's unique circumstances.

Whatever means you choose, the following pages provide thought-starters, examples of things to say, and a few fundamentals about the nature of grief and bereavement. You can apply them in almost any format—be they personal letters, narrative social media posts, or even scripting ideas for making videos.

In the end, compassion can transcend any medium. Use your good judgment for what will be most meaningful at the other end. The key question is "What will the *recipient* prefer?" not "What do *I* prefer?"

Either way, most people will appreciate hearing from you by any means possible.

How Do I Start?

First, relax. Your high school English teacher isn't lurking over your shoulder here, pen poised to strike with the red ink. Nor is your Drama coach. Second, don't concern yourself with the length of the message. A twenty-page epistle or thirty-minute video could be overwhelming, of course, but for the usual intent of sympathy and condolence, you will do best to focus on matters that truly stir you to comment. Then say no more—don't artificially stretch it out.

Simple openings are fine. A message of condolence can begin by plainly acknowledging that you have learned the news and by expressing your feelings. For example:

Dear Pamela,
Only yesterday, I heard that your mother died of a stroke late last month. I had not known she was ill, and I am saddened to learn of her death.

Also, you may wish to portray your circumstances or activities when the news arrived. For instance:

I had just put the children to bed and settled into my evening reading when your brother William called.

The simplicity of these passages conveys more significance than you might think because this can already contribute to the healing process.

Here's how: The death of someone we love frequently evokes a sense of numbness and disorientation, especially if it was unexpected. By briefly describing how you learned of the death and what you were doing at the time, you help the bereaved person perceive this event as happening in other people's lives as well, thus making it more real. When we do this, we validate one another's experience, somewhat like when we exchange details of what we were doing when a tragic public event occurred.

Such descriptions of tangible circumstances help anchor the eerie feelings of great loss into concrete details of time, place, and activity. Do you remember the saying, "Joy shared is multiplied; pain shared is divided?" When you show how the news disrupted what you were doing, if only in a small way, you begin to validate and participate in their loss.

How Can I Elaborate?

Once you begin the letter, conversation, or video, you may wish to mention one or more favorite memories of the deceased. If the memories are meaningful to you, they are capable of enlarging the recipients' awareness of the impact their loved one had on you (and others) during life. Thoughtful reminiscences help paint a mural of scenes from that life and convey deeper appreciation for the survivors' grief. Indeed, in this way, we frequently learn stories about our loved ones that were unknown while they were alive!

In recalling tales of days past, be honest while being kind. Do not exaggerate feelings of loss or sadness beyond what you genuinely feel. A brief, sincere note comforts better than an artificially extended letter or monologue.

Three ways to illustrate how your life was touched are to:

1. Recall the last time you saw the person who has passed away,
2. Reminisce about qualities she or he had that stand out to you; and
3. Describe one or more memorable moments that you had with the deceased.

Examples of Recalling the Last Time:

The last time I saw Ginger, she was playing with the Jefferson kids under the slide at the picnic. She seemed like a woman who was thoroughly enjoying her life and the liveliness of childhood.

❧

I saw Anne just a week before she died. We ran into each other at the cosmetics counter. She simply could not decide which lipstick to get! I never did learn her final choice.

❧

Your dad came by our house three days before Christmas, which is how I'll always remember him. He had a Santa's cap on his head and a briefcase in his hand. "Nerd of the North" he called himself.

Examples of Personal Qualities:

One of the small but vivid things about Franklyn's friendliness was the way he shook hands, with his thumb curved way back, as though even his hand went to extra effort to make me feel welcome.

❧

Most of all, Judy was always kind to me. She loaned me things; she listened to me.

❧

Jamie was one of those rare combinations of beauty and grace. In fact, in my opinion, her gracefulness was the essence of her beauty. She could take a rough comment from a difficult client, re-work it, and offer it right back to him in a way that defused the session's hostility, and sometimes even draw a laugh.

Examples of Memorable Moments:

I remember thirty years ago. You and Felix led the young adolescent group at church in a sex education program. While you took the girls, Felix's calm candor— as well as his tolerance of the boys' giggling and elbowing throughout the film—guided us to valid information and to healthy perspectives that serve me to this day. It's even a legacy now, benefiting the next generation of this household.

❧

Do you remember the summer pool party at the Perrys? Janice slipped and hit her head on the diving board as she fell in. Most of us looked in stunned fascination for a moment, uncertain what to do next. Not Patrick. He instantly dove in, pulled her up, and made sure she wasn't seriously hurt. It's not surprising he went on to become a doctor.

❧

To me, Grandmother was a friend and more. You're too young to remember, but she took me on my first electric street car ride, to my first college football game, and even to my first burlesque show!

You can, of course, combine these illustrations:

Thanksgiving was the last time Rebecca and I had a chance to visit. Her laughter and joking were typical of her great spirit, especially since she already knew her prognosis. Oh, what an example of enduring loveliness.

When Not to Elaborate

Elaborations nearly always enrich the "mural" portrayed above, but they do have limits.

Occasionally, you will find yourself in a situation where such expansion is highly awkward or even impossible. For instance, the bereaved may have been severely estranged from the deceased, or the deceased led such a bitter, abusive, and hateful life that reminiscences aggravate more than help. And how do you reflect on the memories of a stillborn child?

In these cases, you probably would be wise to forego memory lane and, instead, focus on other elements of the letter or script. You could easily go straight from your opening to offering assistance, as described later.

What If I Never Knew the Deceased?

In the event you had not known the deceased but know a survivor, you can refer to impressions the survivor gave you of the deceased or of what the deceased meant to the survivor. For example:

> *It has always been clear to me that your sister both challenged you and loved you. Knowing you as I do, I can imagine you will miss her greatly in both ways.*

❧

> *Emelia, I did not know your father, but I have long observed qualities in your character that surely came from having a caring and concerned family and father.*

Specific examples such as these can have the effect of evoking strong feelings in the bereaved person, like sadness and crying. Except in extreme circumstances this is good. Scenes remembered by a caring friend provide additional perspective on the life of the deceased, demonstrate (again) that the loss is shared, and act as stimulus for further catharsis toward healing.

To understand this fully, it helps to understand the difference between pain and grief. Physical pain is mere sensation—it can be eradicated and is not a requisite experience for recovery. For instance, you can take pain relievers the entire time a broken arm mends, and the arm will heal normally. The pain of grief, on the other hand, is an emotional state that must be worked through—medicate the sorrow away, and it will still be waiting for you when the medication fades. (There may be, of course, special circumstances warranting professionally supervised medication.) There are no short cuts through this experience. Resolution of grief calls for direct acknowledgment of the death, realization of our feelings about it (often numerous and fluctuating), and recognition of how our lives are affected. And time.

We may long for easy coasting, but, for most of us, this is an emotionally vertical climb before it levels off. You provide a few healing footholds when you reinforce the impact of the life now concluded.

Will I Be Cheating If I Use AI?

Will you be cheating if you use ideas from this guide or other resources for coping with bereavement? Most would applaud your desire to send the best condolences possible.

While artificial intelligence (AI) was not used in creating *The Day After the Funeral*, AI technology improves every day. Applications (apps) like ChatGPT, Google Gemini, Microsoft Copilot, Claude, and others offer increasingly human-like writing for a vast array of needs. They can do so with different tones of voice, too. Check it out:

> *Ask an AI app to write a concise summary of any famous novel or movie of your choice. Note the results. Then repeat the request, this time directing AI to express the results in the voice of a famous comedian of your choosing. Note the differences.*

Of course, these apps are not perfect. So, should you involve AI in something so intimate? Is this subject matter a bridge too far for even the cleverest app? You have to answer this question for yourself. How do you feel about it?

Before you answer this question, however, you can test it. If you believe the result of the test to be too cold, simply ignore the AI output. You already have your wits, *The Day After the Funeral*, and perhaps other resources to assist.

If you already know AI is for you, or you are open to trying it, you can test it on a case-by-case basis. Good results can be used. Poor results go no further.

Two simple test strategies are:

1. You write the first draft of the text or the script, then ask the app to polish it. How does the final result look? If you like it, use it. If you are using AI for a letter, you can even write it by hand to increase the personal touch.

2. Inversely, ask the app to draft the first version, then you polish it. You will not have to give the app extraordinary details, but at least indicate you need a message of condolence to [the recipient's name] regarding the late [name of the deceased] and perhaps the relationship between the two—e.g., sister, friend, etc. More details are optional. Perhaps request that the message be less than 200 words or two minutes max.

When the app reveals the draft, it is your turn to refine it. Are there details you need to add or amend? Does certain wording need editing to sound more like you?

Then, how does the final message look? If you like it, thank your app, and use it.

One caveat: If you intend to use AI for 100% of the writing, why send such a message? Do you really care? Remember, not all relationships or circumstances demand your response.

How Else Can I Help?

Often those reaching out to the bereaved will say, "Let me know if there is anything I can do." This is an appealing gesture and is okay as far as it goes, but it often fails to be of real use to survivors.

The days immediately following a death swell with numerous pragmatic matters in addition to the emotional stress. Hence, bereaved persons frequently have a terrific jumble on their minds. They may not be thinking too clearly or decisively, and they may be in no position to coordinate a stream of well-wishers asking to be put to productive use.

What more can you do? First, take the time to think of specific ways you can help and put them in the letter, post, or video. Because you are farther from the turmoil than the family (emotionally and perhaps geographically), you may have a better vantage point for identifying certain actions that preoccupied family members will overlook or feel overwhelmed with.

You can offer to do at least two things that are easily rendered from any distance:

1. Suggest names of people who would want to be notified but whom the family may not immediately know about (e.g., former colleagues, classmates, or distant friends), and

2. Offer to inform widely dispersed groups of the death (e.g., via the newspaper of a town where the deceased grew up or spent many adult years; or via veteran, corporate, civic, union, or professional blogs and newsletters).

Examples of Suggesting Names:

If we don't get in touch with the Johnson City staff, they may be hurt. A few may want to make the drive for the memorial service.

❧

Don't forget Tim, Alice, her brothers and sisters and the Sheinbergs. They would all want to know what happened to Jacques. I'll let them know.

Examples of Informing Groups:

I know lots of alumni/ae from the '74-'78 period would want to know the news. I'd like to write a note to the "Red & Blue" editor.

❧

I'm going to let the brothers at the lodge in Clarksville know, too. He had lots of friends there because of our joint projects.

❧

She must have known half the people in East St. Louis, with all the good she did there. I think submitting some details to their newspaper's online obituary section would be in order.

❧

I'm not sure if members of Springfield's VFW Post got the news. I'll get on the horn with someone there to get the word out. Sammi was a remarkable figure to many there.

Another way to offer assistance flows naturally from the first: ***Just do it!*** If you already know the names of friends or associates who would want to be notified of the death, why not list them in your message? There is no point in delaying until later. Or state that you will proceed to notify news outlets and blogs in towns where the person or family has lived (unless the family requests otherwise).

Other ways to help are open if you live nearby. In this case, you may want to give some thought to the duration of any assistance you propose. Are circumstances and the relationship such that a one-time offer is most appropriate? Or does this situation and your ability to follow through warrant support extending over a period of time?

Here are examples of both:

One Time Only:

If you don't shoo me away, I'm coming over a week from Thursday night and taking the little ones for a pizza party, so you and Pat can have an evening alone.

Extended Offer:

I'd like to make sure we get together at least a couple of times a month for a while. Tuesdays or Saturdays are best for me. If you prefer something else, let me know.

By combining your knowledge of the deceased and survivors with a few moments of creative thinking about their history and circumstances, you likely can generate additional—often unpredictable—ways to help the family. Consider these to stimulate your ingenuity:

- House sit for the family while they are at the funeral or if they need to leave town for a few days afterwards. Thieves often study funeral notices for opportune times to strike a home likely to be unattended.

- In the case of a widowed spouse with young children, help take care of the kids during the first week and/or periodically thereafter.

- If you suspect that the survivors are in disarray about the estate, and you have—or know someone with—special expertise with wills and estate finances, offer to help with these matters. You don't have to be an accountant or estate attorney; knowledgeable lay people can often help a confused family with the basics. Much can be done even when you do not live in the same city. Of course, finances can always be a touchy matter, so approach with tact.

- Send website links having information pertinent to the recipient's circumstances.

- If the deceased was employed at the time of death, help put the family in touch with the organization's benefits manager or human resources (personnel) department to see what benefits may be available for survivors.

- If the family or the deceased actively used a Post Office box, offer to check it regularly for a while. Even offer to send notices of the death to appropriate entities that mail to the box.

- Spouses, parents, or adult children frequently "specialize" in tasks they perform for the household, like mowing the lawn, balancing the checkbook, doing the laundry, bathing the kids, or taking Grandpa for his treatments. Can you pitch in to cover some of these life maintenance tasks for a while? Even if you do it differently (e.g., take the laundry to the cleaners or hire a neighborhood youngster to mow the lawn), you can still relieve survivors of significant burdens until they get new patterns established.

- After a month or more has passed, create a "morale kit" to provide a spontaneously upbeat day. This can include things for various ages, like colorful flowers, magazines or comics, quirky little toys, candles, cookies, funny photos, words-to-live-by posters, stress-relieving bath oil beads, tickets to a ball game, and so forth. And don't forget chocolate.

- Even if you do not take a morale kit, consider visiting a month or so after the funeral—in person or virtually. By then, most of the major commotion has settled down, and the absence and loneliness usually start to become starker. A friendly presence now can be especially valuable.

- One thing you can do in such a visit that is impossible in letters, text posts, and videos: you can listen. Just hush and give the survivor(s) a chance to express themselves if they need to.

The list goes on indefinitely, ever different for different conditions. What needs do you see in the current situation that offer a unique opportunity for you to step forward? Remember, the more helpful the letter, post, or video is to the survivor, the better you are going to feel, too.

Whether you generate many ideas or few, you can always provide details for how to reach you by phone, email, or social media. This is a simple gesture and may not be very necessary in practical terms. Yet it is a symbolic commitment. It punctuates the message with a signal that you are available.

Last, and certainly not least, realize your own limits. If you would be uncomfortable being called upon, do not feel obligated to suggest you are more available than is really the case. That will only complicate your life and the lives of those you wish to comfort.

How Do I Refer to the Deceased?

Simple. Refer to the dead person by name. Do not refer continually to her or him as "the deceased," "the departed," or other nameless pseudonyms.

The person has always been Rasheed or Rebecca or Mikey or whomever, and remains so. Dying does not remove one's name any more than does enrolling in trade school, retiring, or joining a bowling league.

Is There Anything I Should Avoid?

Yes.

When communicating with bereaved family and friends, don't be overly eager to rush them to healing. Healing takes time. It is not appropriate to say, "I know you will be back to normal right away" or to somehow express a need for the hurt to be over in the immediate future. A statement like, "I know I can count on you to recover quickly and be back in top shape Monday morning" is ignorant and cruel.

Also, avoid claims like, "I know just how you feel" or "I know exactly what you're going through." This is especially true for exceptionally traumatic experiences that you have not gone through yourself, like an infant's death or deadly military combat. However, if you have had a similar horrible experience, you may be better suited to extend support and be believed by the recipient.

In either case, the simple truth is you do not know precisely how the other person feels any more than she or he will know your exact feelings when you experience the loss of a loved one. What you may feel, and may safely express, is that you know how you felt when someone particularly close to you died.

For instance:

My brother died when I was fourteen. Hearing of your daughter's death reminded me of my feelings then. I felt so hollowed out.

Expressing parallel feelings will go a long way to establishing the emotional link inherently sought in a statement like "I know how you feel." You need not have identical experiences to appreciate and be appreciated.

Regarding a somewhat different situation, if there is some aspect of the deceased's life or death that was particularly distasteful (e.g., drunk driving that killed the loved one and innocent others), do not feel obligated to mention it for the sake of "total honesty." This is a message of sympathy, not a therapeutic intervention. Substantial difficulties would best be dealt with in another fashion (professional counseling, for example).

Also, be cautious with assurances like "This was God's plan for her" or "He's in a better place now." Usually prompted by the writer's need to show compassion, these phrases are often resented, especially in the early going. They are so easy to say verbally but so hard to accept viscerally, even for someone who eventually comes to find peace in their intent. This being said, do we have to abandon all expressions of faith? Not at all, as you will see in the section *How Do I Talk About Faith*?

How Do I Talk About Faith?

Now we are on hallowed ground, so to speak. Discussing faith with a bereaved person is the best thing you can do. Or the worst.

Adapting to the death of a loved one inherently taps soul-deep places within us. When grounded in a trusting rapport and expressed with humble conviction, sharing your religious or spiritual perspective can hearten the reader at a time when he or she most needs the embrace of the Divine. However, tread cautiously. When religious expressions are forced, patronizing, or condemning, they easily contaminate much of the goodwill otherwise rendered by your efforts.

Let's look at three ways of handling this matter.

First, if you have a conspicuously religious relationship with the reader (formally or informally), giving voice to the power, perspective, and restorative capacity of your faith is a natural extension of your bonds. If the recipient and you have had similar spiritual walks—or even different walks but accepted by one another—go ahead and share images or scriptures that have meaning for you; they have a good chance of being meaningful to your reader. Passages that you already know were particularly favored by the deceased (or the reader) present excellent starting points.

The following passages may help get you going.

An Example Drawn from The Psalms:

Avram, if ever there was a time to fear not while passing through the valley of the shadow of death, this is it. The Creator of the Universe did not make us to be toys for tragedy's capricious folly. Fall towards your remaining family now, not away; we can be your rod and your staff.

One Mindful of Paul's Epistle to the Romans:

You know, at one level, I'm broken and hurting and don't feel like I'll ever get over it. Yet, at another level, I know I have gotten through before, and I keep returning to "neither death, nor life, nor... principalities ... shall be able to separate us from the love of God, which is in Christ Jesus...." The rays of that Love keep glimmering through in my darkest moments.

Another Evoking Hope from the Surah Jonah:

Remember the invitation extended to us to the Home of Peace? I'm confident our friend abides there now in Paradise. I like to think that one day our lives will merit joining him.

The second approach runs directly counter to the first: when it comes to religion, you don't need to bring it up at all. It is not a requirement. If you have no compass for the direction of the reader's spiritual leanings, your thoughts on the

Divine will not be missed. And if you, yourself, are confused, hostile, or uncomfortable with the religious implications of death, why convey a welter of conflicting emotions in a message motivated by the desire to restore and heal?

In some cases, you may know outright that an individual or family prefers agnostic or atheistic understandings. That is their faith, if you will, and talking of God's promises may be easily construed as insensitive disregard for their viewpoint at a vulnerable time, not received as the sanctuary you intend. Faithful people, including missionaries, express care for others all the time without overlaying religious contexts. The letter itself "walks" your conviction; this may not be the best time to "talk" it. Besides, a truly empathic letter is already a powerful form of outreach.

Obviously, the converse holds true for the atheist or agnostic writing to persons of faith. Do not tack on some message about the non-existence of God in a letter meant to render comfort to a believer. Providing an encouraging word can be done while neither eroding your viewpoint nor insincerely parroting other viewpoints you do not share. When in doubt, just don't "go there."

A third, more delicate "middle path" approach can be applied when we want to share spiritual encouragement or insight when someone has a different religion from our own or about whose views we simply have no knowledge.

Don't forget that anyone—devout, atheistic, or agnostic—may be prompted by a death to seek spiritual perspectives from others. If you are called upon, respond candidly yet with humility.

For instance, here an active duty subordinate attempts to address the perennial question, "Why?"

Captain, when we were walking back to the car, you asked, "Why did she have to die this way?" I couldn't think of what to say at the moment. I just knew it was deadly for her and tragic for us. Later, I realized I might have something to offer.

Sir, I can't speak for the Almighty, but I can tell you this. When I've faced the big "Why?" and couldn't answer it directly—which is most of the time—I found my own personal way to answer it indirectly. At least it works for me.

The trick is to find my personal answer to two other questions: First, "What do I understand now that I did not understand before?" The understanding may occur at a mental or emotional level. Or both. Second, "Who can I help or will I help now that I couldn't or wouldn't help before?" When I recognize what I understand more deeply because I've lived through a tragedy or realize who I can reach better, then I usually have my private solution for "why."

Your answer will be different. It's not fancy, but it has helped me weather more than one storm.

This one bravely, yet pastorally, attempts to address the reader about a fear of eternal judgment:

Grace, you said something that I want to respond to. You expressed fear that Joey was destined for hell because he didn't follow certain teachings of the church. Maybe I stand apart from a few famous religious leaders on this point, but in essence, I don't think so.

You know how important my walk with the Lord is to me. I believe God makes all of us certain ways, and Joey couldn't have been a hypocrite any more than he could have grown wings. He was just honest. He worked hard and treated others with respect. He said "I'm sorry" when he was wrong.

He also loved God fiercely, and you know that to be true. Even if you fear that his ways and questions were flaws in the eyes of the Almighty, in my opinion, if they were his only transgressions, then he's going to be in good shape when he applies for admission to the great beyond. He gets a pat on the head and "Well done. You did better than most."

Again, whatever you offer—be it a majority opinion, a minority opinion, or something unique—avoid tones of "I am holier than thou." Please do not proceed as though you are responsible for any conclusions your reader(s) reach. The best any of us can do in these moments is to serve as an instrument, not a final judge. Let it out, lift it up, and let Providence do the rest.

With many survivors, you can use the dynamic suggested earlier when discussing "I know how you feel." That is, rather than tell someone flatly what their religious situation ought to be, share what has had meaning in your life. Simply lay it before the reader as one person who has known pain to another now in pain. For example, here is an excerpt dealing with suicide:

We have never really discussed matters of faith, and I would not want to invade the sanctity of your understandings. Yet, I'd like to share a thought that was tremendously beneficial to me personally after my mother killed herself.

I told a minister friend of another denomination that I feared for the disposition of her soul. Without hesitation, he said that he could not guarantee her status, but "I can tell you I believe in a loving God." Seventeen years later, these words still heal me and give me hope for her well-being. I hope they can provide some assurance to you during this period.

What About Humor?

What about it? Of course, avoid morbid humor or that which is mocking. If joy or laughter were characteristic of the deceased, however, feel free to introduce levity. Being sensitive to the reader does not require a depressive attitude!

A humorous life is unavoidably mourned with touches of mirth. In fact, jovial stories erect sparkling little memorials to joyful times with the one we miss. Any active funeral home director or clergy can tell you of quirky and beneficial humor that has bubbled out during visitations, funerals, and related gatherings. Take this example about a preacher:

> *Who can forget the Sunday that Sonya spoke up during the sermon? You [the widow] and the children were in your usual spot on the pew in front of the pulpit. Emerson had been preaching a short time. Just when he started getting revved up, Sonya [a preschooler] stood up in the pew and proclaimed to Emerson loud enough for all to hear "Sit DOWN, Daddy! You've said ENOUGH!"*
>
> *What part of that day's message do you think everyone remembers the most?*

And here's a PG rated example from college life:

> *Adam was always such a good sport. Did he ever tell you about the stunt we pulled on him our freshman year? The caper was based on having Adam scare our dorm's resident advisor. Our bath facilities were at the*

end of the hall, and every night the RA would go brush his teeth just before going to bed. Adam's assignment was to sneak into the closet during that interlude, then wait until the RA returned and turned off his light. At that point, Adam was to leap out of the closet to terrify our RA.

What Adam didn't know was that we already had someone in the closet waiting for him!! The RA put us up to the whole thing to begin with! The shriek that followed Adam's discovery that he was not alone was phenomenal. As you can guess, he didn't hold a grudge like some guys would have.

So, feel free to share comical incidents that involved the deceased. Kindly comedy reminds the reader of a wonderful fact of life: even though loved ones die, laughter does not die with them.

Dare I Use the "D" Word?

Many people express ambivalence about how to refer to death itself. We feel compelled to use phrases like "passed," "passed away," "going to his Maker," "the great divide," and so forth, in lieu of the words "died," "dying," and "death." The euphemisms are not *wrong* to say; it is just not necessary to use them relentlessly. Indeed, complete avoidance of the latter terms suggests an unwillingness to acknowledge the occurrence of this very real event.

However generous in intent, this avoidance tends to confuse kindness with concealment. By all means share your concern for the bereaved; offer kindness; be of assistance where possible; but do not think you accomplish these goals by avoiding mention of you-know-what. Use of explicit terms befits a message of condolence. As indicated earlier, specific references, more than hinting generalities, evoke release and healing.

This is not difficult. It is as easy as simply saying, "His death came as such a shock to me" or "When I found out Eleanor had died, I wanted to cry. I *did* cry!" or "I knew Toni Jo was dying and thought of her often. I regret that I was unable to travel that far for the funeral."

Sometimes reluctance to use explicit references to death comes down to this: even though such references are honest, specific, and objective, they are not particularly poetic, up-lifting, or spiritually meaningful. The intention of using explicit references is to convey that you know the death took place and, yes, you are comfortable calling it by name. The intention is *not* to ban all possible use of lyrical expression and imagery.

In fact, the most nurturing effect often results when blending the two. The letter in which you explicitly mention death frees up metaphorical language to do its work unencumbered—it does not have to serve as a Trojan horse for concealed messages. The inspirational turn of phrase can then draw up sustenance from wellsprings unreachable by ordinary language.

Perhaps these illustrations will help:

Julius's death ripped wide a curtain concealing a chamber in my heart that I had forgotten was there. I was forced to stare upon memories that I need to share with you when we get together.

❧

The gate is closed for now, the castle bridge drawn. However grieved, we dare not force ourselves across that moat before our own appointed times. Death does that. Yet, even as we speak such things, we enjoy sharing the tales of his wit, his joy, his counsel. We cannot help it. Life does that.

❧

Who really knows what happens when we die? Personally, I do not think it is all about dust-to-dust. For someone like Johnny, especially, I think it is a great deal more about caterpillar-to-monarch butterfly or clay vessel-to-celestial being. Perhaps he'll alight upon our shoulders one unsuspecting afternoon, and we'll grin unconsciously recalling his colorful nature.

By the way, if you find yourself haunted by a vague pressure to write something more exotic than is natural for you, remember that some people have the gift for elegant writing and the rest of us do not. Resist coercing yourself to craft artificially ornate scenes or evoke profoundly emotional responses. This is not a Hollywood screen play seeking an envelope at the Academy Awards. This is you talking to a friend. Be yourself.

How Do I Finish?

You can conclude the same way you started—that is, plainly and simply. If this letter, post, or video is the only contact you will have for the foreseeable future, let them know you will be thinking of (or praying for) them, and express a wish for their healing or "returning to peace as time permits." Some people effectively punctuate the conclusion with "I shall miss her" (or him).

If you expect to have, or want to encourage, further interaction, invite the reader to contact you "after life settles down again." Better yet, tell them you will call in the near future to set a lunch date or other suitable visit. Personal visits are special, but virtual visits can accomplish a great deal, too. As mentioned earlier, however, do not make an offer you do not genuinely mean or which would actually make you feel awkward.

What is an appropriate closing for a message of condolence? Should it be "Love" or "Warmly" or "In deepest sympathy?" To answer this question, reflect inwardly a moment on the value of your relationship with the recipient. Then, like a mirror reflecting sunlight onto wounds, have the courage to express the gentlest version of the truth. Also, have equal courage not to overstate what is really in your heart. The wounds of grief can prompt even the toughest personality to appreciate loving thoughts; at the same time, grief rarely makes anyone appreciate fictitious sentimentality. Once again, sincerity paves the way.

And that's it. You have performed a healing, perhaps inspiring, act by writing your letter, sharing your post, or creating a special video. If it says what you had hoped to express and no more, you can be content in contributing to another person's restoration. You will not single-handedly heal them, but you will have contributed another stepping stone on their path to recovery.

Without pretense you have put tangible evidence of care into someone's life while they cope with one of the most painful experiences a human being can endure ... evidence they can appreciate again and again.

How Do I Pull It All Together?

As you start, you might find it helpful to simply create a list of things you want to touch upon. Do not attempt a flawless message off the top of your head. As for ideas and examples provided thus far, use them like a cafeteria, not ingredients in a strict recipe. If one ingredient from a recipe goes unused there can be glaring consequences. But at a cafeteria, you take what you want and whatever you choose is the whole meal. If you take something from every section fine, but if you do not, you're still fine.

Once your key points are in mind, you can certainly present them in the sequence suggested in this guide. However, feel free to move things around. Your style and the various thoughts and feelings you want to express will provide the flow.

Here are a few final examples of entire messages showing how various pieces can appear when put together. We begin with this short note, suitable for writing inside a sympathy card or a media post:

Dear Ms. Smith,

I just wanted to add a note to let you know how much I have always appreciated you and Mr. Smith. Now that he is gone, I shall miss him sorely. Yet, I'll count on still appreciating you.

Until next week, Joni

Next, this thorough message pertains to tragic circumstances and went from two people to an entire family:

Dear Alonzo, May, TR, and Beth,

When we checked our feeds Saturday and saw the story about the accident, we were stunned. We still can't believe it.

Three weeks ago, Chrissie was telling us all about her trip to Ottawa and now this horrible wreck. We shall miss her terribly; we can only imagine your feelings at this moment.

Nothing can erase the pain, but we may be able to help in a small way. Chrissie's aquarium and terriers will need looking after. We'll see to them the next couple of weeks until you decide their future. If needed, we'll be glad to find them new homes but will hold off unless you give the word.

For now, please know that your sorrow is shared.

Most sincerely, Jim and Bertha

This one is classic:

My Dear Monique,

I was weeding the garden when Anna came by to tell me that your father had died. I am so sorry for your loss.

The last time I saw him was at the restaurant. He had that vivid turquoise-handled walking stick with him. I don't know which held him up more—the physical cane or his pride in its craftsmanship.

He was always one for quality. He may have been an aggravation at times, but no one can question his concern for his shop and for customers receiving good work for their dollar. Occasionally, I see his craftsmanship in you, and it is becoming.

God is with us, Monique. Let's give Him a chance to refresh our souls; next week I'll come by and we'll go for a hike on Hummingbird Trail. We can talk, say nothing, cry, laugh, whatever you like. Probably we will do ALL of them.

Also, let me know when I can give you a hand around the house or yard.

That's it for now. See you soon.

Your buddy, Wendy

I'm All Done, Right?

Well, maybe.

With some relationships, you may determine that you have more than one message to send. And the others may be more significant than the first. Fortunately, they are also do-able long after the funeral if you were unable to send something sooner.

For starters, mark the first anniversary of the death on your calendar. Next year, as that date approaches, send a message to the appropriate survivors (or survivor) letting them know you are thinking of them as that day approaches. Most often, people say something about "keeping you in our thoughts and prayers" as the anniversary of the death draws near. Since that phrase can be overused, also consider alternatives like, "We are remembering you with fondness" (or "with love" or "with admiration," or "We continue to lift you up for peace and healing."). Here's an example:

Dear Mrs. McGregor,
As the first year since Mr. McGregor's death comes to an end, we'd like for you and the family to know that we are thinking of you this week. We still miss him. He was so much fun.
Please know that our prayers surround you all.
With warmest regards,

Count on it. Survivors will be aware of the anniversary, consciously or unconsciously. It is not uncommon for survivors to feel sad a year later and be mystified why they are in a slump. Then they realize they are on or near the anniversary date of the loved one's death. (Maybe this has happened to you.)

Similarly, there will be other emotional spikes during the year that vary for different individuals. As the year rolls around, consider sending a message at one or more of the following times: the next birthday of the deceased; Mother's/Father's Day the year a parent passed away; at graduation time a senior would have celebrated; the Memorial Day following an active duty service member's or veteran's death; religious holidays significant to the deceased; and other dates you know that are significant to the survivor(s).

Recipients may be amazed that you remembered, touched that you cared to reach out again, and particularly grateful that someone still kept them in mind so long after the funeral. A year later, yours may be the lone embrace they receive.

Who Can Use This Book?

In addition to the natural circle of friends and family, there are numerous capacities in which professionals, lay people, and volunteers may find themselves in need of this assistance. Here are just a few for whom *The Day After the Funeral: What to Say to Those Who Grieve* could be ideal:

- Hospices, for...
  All members of the care team, clinical
      and administrative
  Volunteer training
  Community education

- Funeral homes, for...
  Visitation guests
  Funeral service guests
  Staff members

- Bereavement support groups, for...
  Group members
  Visitors
  Public education

- Clergy of all faiths, for...
  Direct personal and professional use
  Lay care-giving training
  Seminary and college students
  Judicatory/denominational offices

- Psychological, psychiatric and counseling professionals, for...
  Direct personal and professional use
  Workshops and seminars
  Supplemental resource material for clients/patients

- Extended care and nursing home facilities, for...
  Residents' friends and families
  Clinical staff members
  Adjunct staff members

- Hospitals, for ...
  Clinical and administrative staff
  Chaplains
  Social workers
  Gift shops

- And a wide range of special uses like veteran's groups, nurse oncology associations, life insurance agents, financial advisors, greeting card stores, and florists.

Nearly all of these groups have national, state, or local organizations that may want to make this resource known to their members.

This list is hardly exhaustive. In the end, who *won't* find themselves befriending someone surviving great loss? If that act of friendship takes the form of a written or video message, hopefully this guide has been of service to you.

A Final Word

Sharing a message of comfort to someone who is grieving comes naturally for some and agonizingly for others. To the former, congratulations. What may seem so simple to you is in fact a singular gift for reaching beyond yourself.

To the latter, have courage. Do not feel forced into something that causes you tremendous anxiety. After all, condolence cards and sympathy memes are available to you. If you like, you can combine your personal sentiments with a card or meme, creating an inspiring blend.

Either way, try not to resist the generous impulse. Would you rather send your best and have someone interpret an imperfect message...or send nothing at all and have them interpret the silence?

Acknowledgments

Thanks to the still, small voice that urged me to contact Rev. Dale Clem regarding a writing project. Thanks to Dale for his encouragement and introducing me to editor and publisher Chris Angermann of Bardolf & Company. And a major "thank you" to Chris for his guidance in bringing this new, improved edition to reality with his keen writing insights and knowledge of today's publishing landscape.

Thanks, too, to the late Norma Wylie, MSN, Professor Emerita of Southern Illinois University School of Medicine and author of *Sharing the Final Journey*, who was my mentor and friend in matters of loss adjustment. By discourse and by example, she taught that the best way to face grief is with all your heart, mind, and soul. And a touch of humor doesn't hurt.

I am grateful to several others, as well. For their reviews and recommendations, my sincere appreciation goes to: my friend and colleague on the team establishing North Alabama's first hospice, Ms. Carolyn Loshuertos; the Reverends Frank Broyles, Bob Loshuertos, and Jim Norris, clergy of different stripes; Dr. Richard Moore, the English professor I asked to look over my shoulder; the late Rev. Houston Hodges, author, pastor, and chronic encourager; my lovely wife Adrianne, master of detail and constant

support; Sheryl Fullerton, editorial advisor adding profes-
sionalism with grace; and longtime friend and author Alan
Briskin, helping to steward this to success.

Ordering Information

To order additional copies of *The Day After the Funeral*,
singly or in bulk, contact your favorite book store, online
site, or:

Bardolf & Company
Tel. 941-232-0113
www.bardolfandcompany.com

About the Author

John Haley received his Master's Degree from the University of Illinois-Springfield with a major emphasis in Clinical Thanatology (Death, Dying and Bereavement). His studies included a year of Clinical Pastoral Education (CPE) through a joint program with the Southern Illinois University School of Medicine and St. John's Catholic Hospital.

He returned to Huntsville, Alabama, where he helped establish the region's first hospice program and served as its founding vice president. Thereafter, he pursued a career in organizational development and training in other venues, including medical, educational, religious, manufacturing, and governmental.

John has previously published on this topic in professional, charitable, and religious periodicals.

www.ingramcontent.com/pod-product-compliance
Lightning Source LLC
Chambersburg PA
CBHW051432270326
41934CB00019B/3488